Ah, Music!

Written and Illustrated by *Aliki*

HARPERCOLLINSPUBLISHERS

*Where there is life,
there is music*

(speech bubble: Music is a universal language.)

A Prelude

Only once have I ever heard someone say he had no music in his life. He is a lonely exception. Most everyone else seems to have a connection.

My own introduction began as a child of Greek immigrants, when my family converged on Sundays to make music together. Grandparents, parents, uncles, aunts, and cousins danced, sang in rich harmony, and played old and new world instruments—bouzouki, mandolin, guitar, accordion, harmonica, cello, violin, and piano—in their "orchestra." At three, I sang Greek folk song solos, propped up on a table by my aunt, and picked out on the piano any tune I heard on the radio.

Music flowed through our elementary and high schools, where it was an integral part of education. Band, orchestra, choir, chorus, glee club— we had it all.

At home, each of us studied piano. Besides that, one sister also studied cello and dance, the other voice, my brother "played the radio," and mine was tuned to the classical station as I drew. On long family drives, it was as natural as could be for us to burst into a Bach chorale, or the Hallelujah chorus in four parts. We were united in music.

Ah, Music! Copyright © 2003 by Aliki Brandenberg Manufactured in China. All rights reserved. No part of this book may be used or reproduced in any manner whatsoever without written permission except in the case of brief quotations embodied in critical articles and reviews. For information address HarperCollins Children's Books, a division of HarperCollins Publishers, 195 Broadway, New York, NY 10007. www.harperchildrens.com

Library of Congress Cataloging-in-Publication Data
Aliki.
 Ah, music! / Written and illustrated by Aliki.
  p. cm.
 Summary: Surveys the history and components of music, concentrating on Western musical traditions.
 ISBN 0-06-028719-5 — ISBN 0-06-028727-6 (lib. bdg.) — ISBN 0-06-446236-6 (pbk.)
 1. Music—History and criticism—Juvenile literature. [1. Music—History and criticism.] I. Title.
ML3928 .A45 2003
780—dc21   2001026476
                                                                                                                          CIP AC

Typography by Al Cetta
18 SCP 20 19 18 17 16
❖

*For Willa Demetria
With a song in my heart*

With Thanks

Over three years ago, the piecing together of words and pictures for this book began. (The idea had yeasted for years before.) Since then, I have been inundated with books, radio, TV, films, concerts, and people who helped, guided, inspired, or gave a mere word. Grateful thanks to each and every one of them.

Especially, my thanks to Phoebe Yeh for her constant care and support, Al Cetta for his usual patience and skill, Renée Cafiero for her microscopic observations, and Whitney Manger and Drew Willis for being there.

To Robert Waldman (composer, New York) for his friendship and musicianship. To Jeremiah W. McGrann (Assistant Professor, Boston College, Massachusetts), Rob Roman (San José Jazz Society, California), and Michael Mulder (P.S. 183, New York City), for their valuable suggestions.

To Pete Bergeron and Mike McClowskey (New Orleans, Louisiana) for that intensive session on local music at Mulate's (not yet founded in "1900"!).

To Martina Thomson (London) for her keen eye, Esther Hautzig (New York City) for digging, and Leila and Emma Schütz (Paris) for playing for me.

To wonderful LeeAnn Lugar (William E. Miller Elementary, Ohio) for keeping her students alive with music, Rachel Powell (Valley Forge Elementary, Pennsylvania) who said "a cappella," Mary Kepple (Wiggin Street Elementary, Ohio), who was teaching a canon, and to all those unnamed who listed their favorite popular music.

Thanks to Maestro Leonard Slatkin for his music, sensitivity, humor, and timely BBC Radio music lecture series, and Wynton Marsalis for his enthusiastic televised Jazz series for children of all ages.

Most of all, deepest thanks to R. Vivian Walton (Yeadon High School, Pennsylvania), who filled her students with a love of music for a lifetime.

Ah, Music!

CONTENTS

What is Music?	6
Music is Sound	7
Rhythm	8
Melody	9
Pitch and Tone	10
Volume	11
Feeling	12
A Creative Art	14
The Written Music	15
The Creation Comes to Life	16
Instruments	18
Conductor	21
Voice	22
Harmony	24
Dance	26
History of Music	30
Prehistoric	30
Ancient	31
Early	33
Classical	34
Diversity of Music	38
Jazz	40
Popular	42
Therapy	44
Practice Makes Perfect	46

What is Music?

Music is Sound

If you hum a tune,

play an instrument,

or clap out a rhythm,

you are making music.
You are listening to it, too.

Music is Rhythm

That is the beat I can clap.

Rhythm is a marching-band beat, a puffing-train beat,

a beating-the-eggs beat, a heart beat.
Some rhythm beats are stronger than others.
You can count the accents.

A person who cannot hear
can feel the vibration of the beat.

Music is Melody

That is the tune I can hum,

or the song that is sung
if words are set to music.
Often the words are poetry.

Music is Pitch and Tone

Pitch is the highs and the lows of the sound.
Tone is the color—the brightness or darkness of the sound.
Some instruments have a high, bright pitch.

High, sharp pings can sound like piercing light.

Some instruments have a deep, low pitch.
They can sound dark, shadowy, and mysterious.

Music is Volume

That is the loudness or the softness of the sound.

Shhhh.

Music is Feeling

It sets a mood.

Music speaks not with words, as in a song.
It speaks with expression.
It is a universal language that unites people.
Everyone can understand music, because everyone has feelings.
Music can make you feel happy or sad or scared.
It can make you want to dance, to march, to sing,
or to be quiet, to listen, and to dream.

Ah, music!

*Here will we sit
and let the sounds of music
creep in our ears.*

Shakespeare said that.

I listen to music,
and I can see pictures in my head.

I imagine I hear twittering birds.

I hear a cool waterfall.

I see a brilliant sunrise.

I see a scary dark forest.

I hear a noisy city.

Music is a Creative Art

Just as a writer uses words,

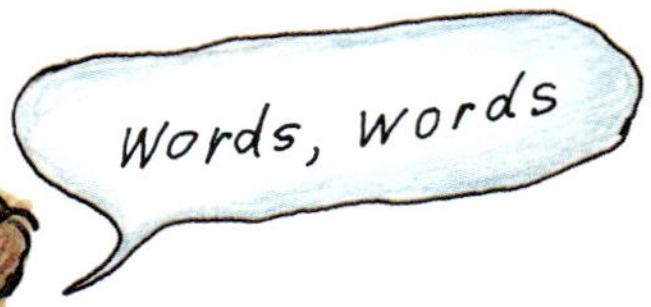

Words, words

or an artist uses paint,

a composer uses music
to create images and feelings.
He writes it down in notes, symbols,
and numbers on lines and spaces.
The notations describe the rhythm, tone, pitch,
feeling, and even the silences of the piece.

Wolfgang Amadeus Mozart wrote his first composition when he was five years old.

I'd better get busy!

The Written Music

Every note shows its time value.
Some notes are long. Some are short.
Every note's placement on the staff shows a pitch value.
Symbols show pauses, and how loud, soft, fast,
or slow the notes are played.

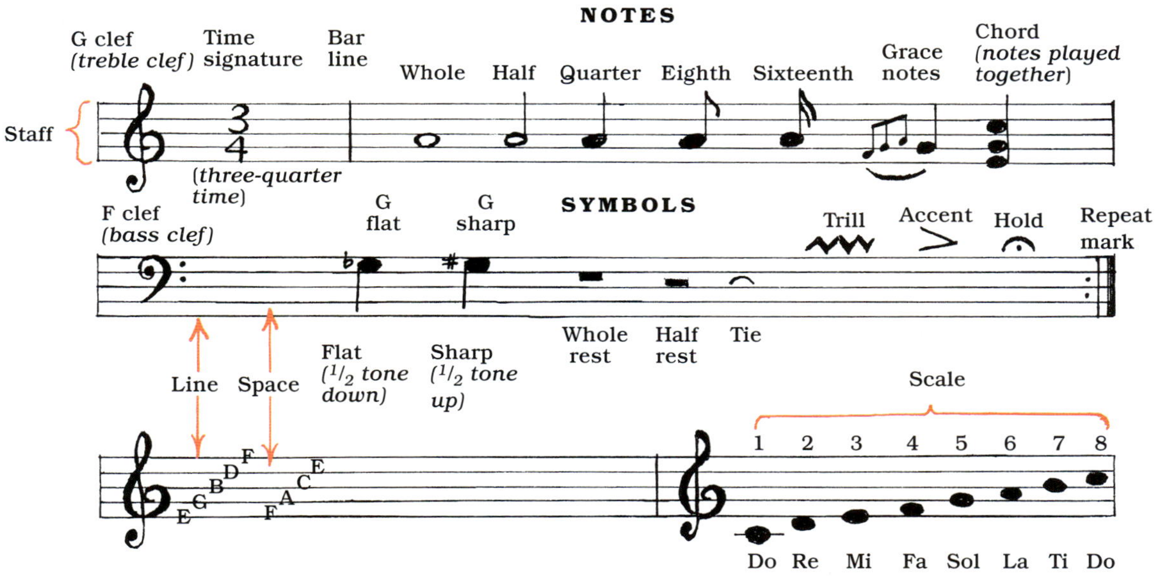

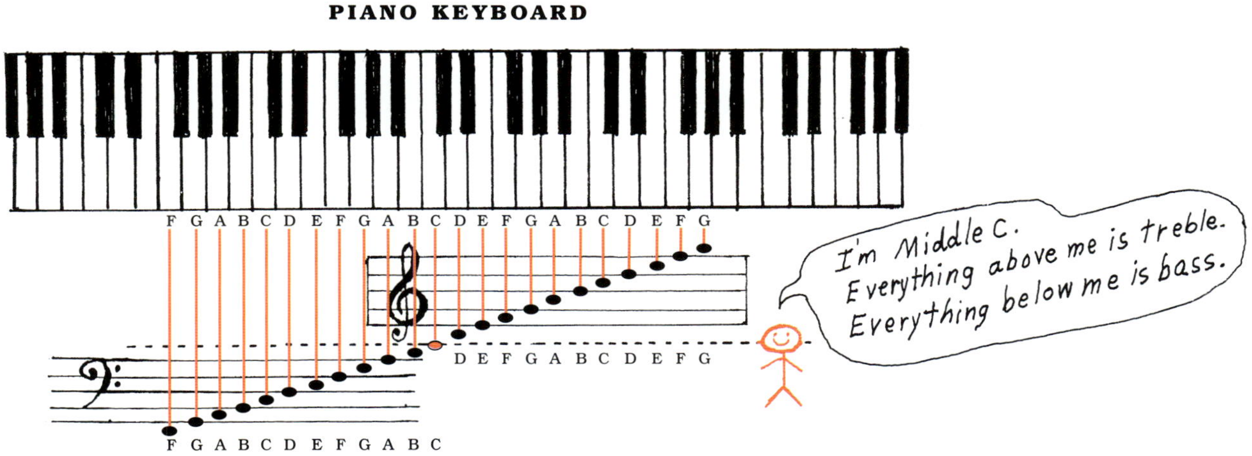

Reading the written music is like reading a composer's handwriting.

Bach   Mozart   Bartók

The Creation Comes to Life

A musician will perform the composition.
She will bring to life the composer's written work.

She reads the music and studies it.

She practices the piece
on her instrument, the cello.

The instrument makes the sound,
and gives the music color.
The musician puts her own feeling
into the music too.
At last, she is ready to perform
the piece for others to enjoy.

Music is composed for one instrument,

Solo

for a group of instruments,

Trio

Chamber music is played by two to ten musicians in a room or small, intimate hall.

or for a whole orchestra.

An orchestra plays in a large auditorium. Some music has been written for over one hundred instruments, and even a chorus—all playing and singing together as a team. It is a thrilling sound.

Some Instruments of the Orchestra

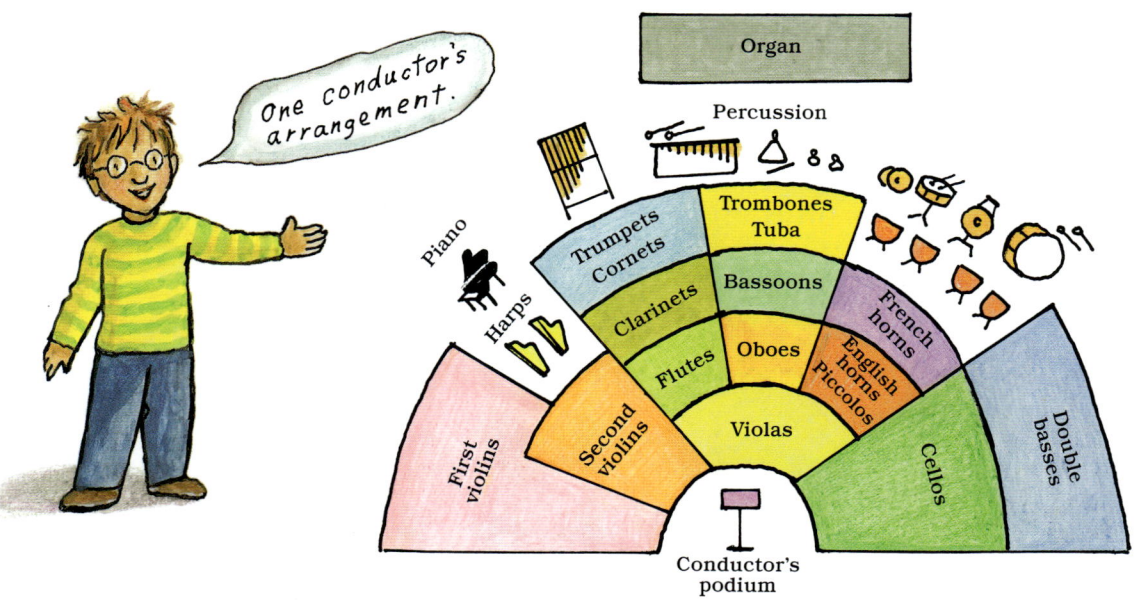

One conductor's arrangement.

STRINGED INSTRUMENTS

Played with a bow, or plucked or strummed. The strings vibrate to make the sound.

Violin

Viola

Cello

Double bass

Bow

Piano
Keys hit the strings inside.

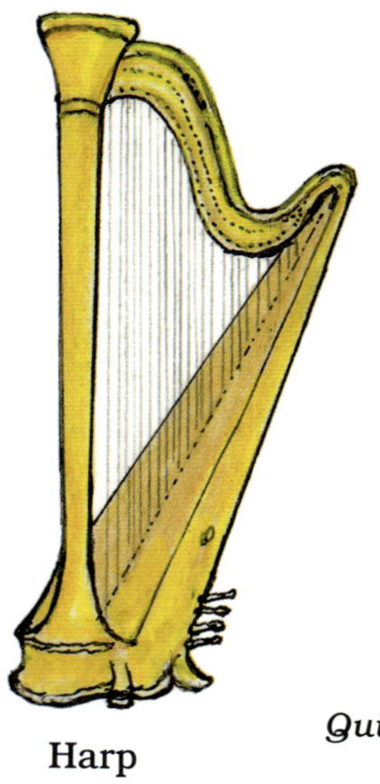

Harp

Harpsichord
Quills pluck the strings inside.

Guitar

Plectrum
to pluck with

Lute

Mandolin

18

WIND INSTRUMENTS

*Woodwinds and brass are blown to make the sound.
Sound vibrates inside a hollow tube.*

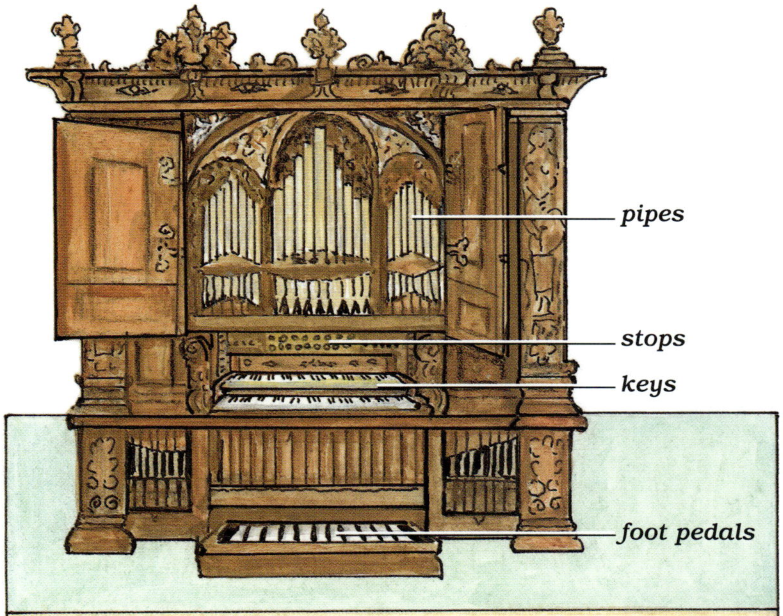

WOODWINDS

Hands and feet pump air into organ pipes to change the sounds. A large organ may be built directly into an auditorium, cathedral, church, or synagogue.

Organ *(Baroque)*

Flute
Air blown across hole.

Piccolo

The baby of the orchestra

Reed Instruments
Air blown through reed mouthpiece.

Clarinet

Oboe

Saxophone
Unique reed instrument

English horn

Bassoon

Double bassoon

BRASS

Air blown into metal mouthpiece.

Cornet

Bugle

Trombone

Trumpet

French horn

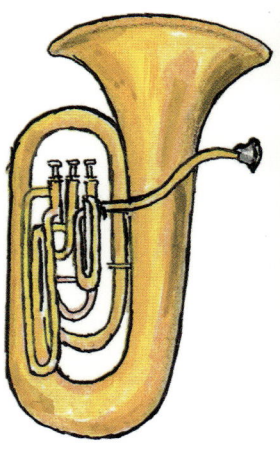

Tuba

19

The Conductor

A conductor, or maestro, leads the orchestra. Some conductors hold a baton.

He follows the score, which shows all the instrumental and vocal parts of the piece.
The maestro signals the musicians when to start, stop, to play louder, softer, faster, or slower.
He directs them with feeling.
Each instrument is unique and important, whether it is played alone or with others.
It is the musicians who make the instruments come alive, and they do their very best.

The Voice is an Instrument Too

All kinds of music have been composed for one or more voices. Popular songs, spirituals, jazz, Lieder, opera, musicals, and choral music tell stories in both words and music.

Popular songs, Ballads

Jazz, Blues, Spirituals

Lieder (German songs)

Opera

Musicals, Operettas

Chorus, Choir, Glee club

Children's choir

Singers' voices have different pitches.
Women's voices can reach higher.
Men's voices can reach lower.

Children's voices are high.

Soprano is very high.

Alto is lower.

Tenor is lower.

Bass is way down lowest.

And some voices are even higher and in between.

Mezzo soprano

Counter tenor

Bass baritone

Or lower. CROAK!

Music is Harmony

Harmony is the sound of different notes that blend together.

Now Let's Count!

ONE is a solo.
TWO, a duet.
THREE is a trio.
FOUR, a quartet.
FIVE is a quintet.
SIX, a sextet.
SEVEN is a septet. *But we don't fit!*

Dynamics, Tempo, and Italian

Musical terms are expressed in Italian. *Si, si.*

Dynamics is the softness or loudness of the music.

pp	**p**	**mp**	**mf**	**f**	**ff**
pianissimo	*piano*	*mezzopiano*	*mezzoforte*	*forte*	*fortissimo*
(very soft)	(soft)	(medium soft)	(medium loud)	(loud)	(very loud)

Tempo is the slowness or quickness of the music.

Largo	*Adagio*	*Andante*	*Moderato*	*Allegro*	*Vivace*	*Presto*
(very slow)	(slow)	(walking)	(medium)	(fast)	(fast and lively)	(very fast)

Music is to Dance to

GOTTA DANCE!

When I hear the beat,
I can't control my feet.
I tap, I stamp, I whirl, I fly.
I'm free as a leaf. That's why!

All over the world, people dance for fun, in performance, to express themselves, or to tell a story.
Whatever the dance form—classical ballet, modern, tap, religious, popular, or folk—dancers use their bodies to express the music.

Ballet

Modern dance

Tap

Square dance

Ballroom dance

Jazz
(The Charleston)

Ice dance

Stomp

Flamenco
(Spain)

27

Earliest Music

Prehistoric

Music making began thousands of years ago. When people celebrated a hunt, signaled dangers, worshiped, or told stories, they danced, clapped, banged on hollow logs, shook pebbles, and chanted. Later, they made primitive instruments from stone, bone, shells, and metal that archaeologists would discover. Variations of some are used even today.

Seed-filled gourd rattle
2000 B.C.

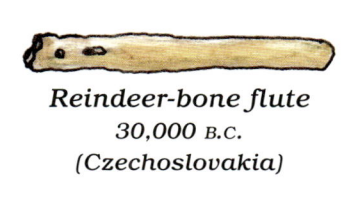

Reindeer-bone flute
30,000 B.C.
(Czechoslovakia)

Skin-covered drum

Bone signal whistle
40,000 B.C.
(Moravia)

Earthenware rattle
(Mexico)

Conch shell horn

Trumpet
Bronze Age

Ancient Music

2600 – 400 B.C.

11-string lyre
2600 B.C.
Mesopotamia (Iraq)

Dancer with cymbals
1400 B.C.
(Egypt)

9-string harp
1400 B.C.
(Egypt)

Throughout the ancient world, music became part of religious rituals and military ceremonies, festivals and entertainment.
Egyptians danced to harps and cymbals.
Since biblical times Jews have blown the shofar—one of the oldest instruments in continuous use.
The Chinese had orchestras of bells, gongs, drums, and zithers, and invented a form of written music.

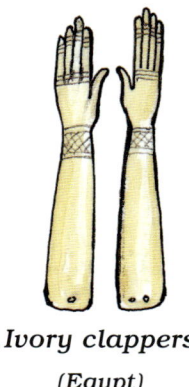

Ivory clappers
(Egypt)

Mayan trumpeter
1500 B.C.
(Mexico)

Cornu (bronze horn)
(Rome)

Shofar (ram's horn)

Po-chung bell
(China)

Music of the Gods

500 – 400 B.C.

In ancient Greece people loved music.
Great thinkers said it was important for body and soul.
Music was woven into every part of daily life—
work, play, theater, sports, and religion.
People danced, sang, piped the aulos, strummed the lyre,
and chanted magical myths about their gods and goddesses.
We have to guess how it sounded, as there is no record
of the written music.

7-string lyre

Dancer

Panpipes (named for Pan, the god of nature)

Double aulos (reed flute)

In 500 B.C., Pythagoras proved through mathematics that vibrations cause the pitch and tone of sound.

Music through the Ages

1st–15th Centuries A.D.

In 1030 an Italian monk, Guido d'Arezzo, devised the basis of the music notation system we still use—with staffs, lines, spaces, and notes.

Music grew from one century to the next. In the early and middle ages, new forms of music developed. Christianity inspired church music. Music became polyphonic—played and sung in two or more melodic parts. Notations were invented. Music was no longer a one-time performance. Now it would be written and preserved for other musicians and generations.

Minstrels in England wandered the streets singing and strumming.

drums   fiddle   bells

Masked musicians, singers, and dancers acted out plays.

Troubadours in France traveled from palace to palace to entertain the courts with romantic ballads.

New instruments, such as the portative organ, were invented.

pipe drum   viol   shawm
bass recorder   harp

Musicians played assorted instruments in groups.

The Flowering of Classical Music

15th – 21st Centuries

My favorite kind.

In the centuries that followed, music in the Western world burst with new inventions and rich complex sounds. Each period of music reflected the changing life and art of its own time.

RENAISSANCE
(1430 – 1600)

Early composers emerge. Notations, as well as the first printed music in 1472, spread their influences across France, Germany, Holland, and England. Choral music dominates.

COMPOSERS:

Dufay (c. 1400–1474)
Josquin des Prez (c. 1445–1521)
Tallis (1505–1585)
Palestrina (1525–1594)
Byrd (1543–1623)

Guillaume Dufay, French master of polyphony and musician who influenced his contemporaries.

Thomas Tallis composed a motet for forty separate voices in England.

Giovanni Palestrina was a master composer of sacred music in Italy.

BAROQUE PERIOD
(1600 – 1750)

Intricate polyphonic music for church, opera, voices, dance, and drama. The organ and new instruments—keyboards, violin, cello, woodwinds— are played solo, in small groups, or in large orchestral groups.

COMPOSERS:

Monteverdi (1567–1643)
Lully (1632–1687)
Buxtehude (1637–1707)
Purcell (1659–1695)
A. Scarlatti (1660–1725)
Couperin (1668–1733)
Vivaldi (1678–1741)
Rameau (1683–1764)
J. S. Bach (1685–1750)
Handel (1685–1759)

Johann Sebastian Bach, organist and one of the greatest composers ever, had 21 children—many of them musicians.

King Louis XIV of France (1643–1715) allowed music, dance, and drama to flourish in his court.

Antonio Stradivarius of Italy (1644–1737) made the finest violins and cellos, still treasured today.

George Frideric Handel's hundreds of dramatic works include the oratorio Messiah.

CLASSICAL PERIOD
(1750 – 1825)

The height of classical music: strong melodies, complex symphonies for large orchestras, concertos for perfected solo instruments. Musicians are employed by the church or by royalty.

COMPOSERS:

Haydn (1732–1809)
Mozart (1756–1791)
Beethoven (1770–1827)
Rossini (1792–1868)
Schubert (1797–1828)

Wolfgang Amadeus Mozart, *regarded by many as the greatest musical genius, lived a short but full and prolific life.*

Franz Josef "Papa" Haydn *wrote hundreds of memorable works and was Mozart's respected friend.*

Ludwig van Beethoven *wrote symphonic masterpieces even after he became deaf.*

Franz Schubert *composed symphonies and over 600 unforgettable Lieder in his brief 31 years of life.*

ROMANTIC PERIOD
(1825 – 1900)

Music becomes descriptive and melodious. It expresses emotion, adventures, beauty of nature, love, tragedy. Great pianists travel abroad to perform concerts.

COMPOSERS:

Berlioz (1803–1869)
Mendelssohn (1809–1847)
Chopin (1810–1849)
Schumann (1810–1856)
Liszt (1811–1886)
Wagner (1813–1883)
Verdi (1813–1901)
Brahms (1833–1897)
Puccini (1858–1924)

Johannes Brahms *is revered for his symphonies, chamber music, and his German Requiem.*

Frédéric Chopin *composed and played moody, complex études, preludes, & nocturnes for the piano.*

Franz Liszt *was both composer and brilliant pianist-performer with a flair for showmanship.*

Richard Wagner, *composer and dramatist, based his long theatrical operas on Germanic legends.*

35

Sound Breaks Through

Like a burst of brilliant fireworks, two inventions in America rocked the world and would change it forever.

Hello, hello? Can you hear me? In 1876, sound is transmitted by telephone.

And in 1877, recorded sound is transmitted. It will bring music and new inspiration to all the world.

It made me famous too!

Alexander Graham Bell *(1847–1922) invented the telephone.*

Thomas Alva Edison *(1847–1931) invented the phonograph.*

NATIONALISM
(1875 – 1900)

A new mixed flavor of music by composers from various countries reflects their homelands, history, folk music, and fairy tales. The great invention of recorded sound will bring music to everyone.

COMPOSERS:

Smetana (1824–1884)
Borodin (1833–1887)
Bizet (1838–1875)
Tchaikovsky (1840–1893)
Dvořák (1841–1904)
Grieg (1843–1907)
Elgar (1857–1934)
Mahler (1860–1911)
Debussy (1862–1918)
Sibelius (1865–1957)
Ravel (1875–1937)

Peter Ilyich Tchaikovsky *composed rich, melodious Russian orchestral music for dance.*

French composer **Georges Bizet**'s *popular opera* Carmen *had a Spanish theme.*

Gustav Mahler, *Austrian composer-conductor, wrote ten intense symphonies.*

Claude Debussy *reflected French Impressionism in his music with color & rhythm.*

Jean Sibelius *described his homeland, Finland, in tone poems & symphonies.*

Enrico Caruso *(1873–1921), Italian-American tenor, became first popular recording artist.*

REVOLUTIONARY TIMES
(1900 – 1940)

New sounds, discord, war, and influences from Russia and the New World. American composers create original music that reflects their cities, lives, and jazz rhythms. Many composers write music for the new art form of cinema.

COMPOSERS:

R. Strauss (1864–1949)
Rachmaninov (1873–1943)
Schoenberg (1874–1951)
Ives (1874–1954)
Stravinsky (1882–1971)
Prokofiev (1891–1953)
Hindemith (1895–1963)
Gershwin (1898–1937)
Weill (1900–1950)
Shostakovich (1906–1975)

Sergei Rachmaninov, *Russian pianist, wrote romantic, melodious music.*

Sergei Prokofiev *expressed Russian experiences and stories in his music.*

Igor Stravinsky *startled the world with rhythmic neoclassical sounds.*

Arnold Schoenberg *found a new form of expression using a 12-tone system.*

Kurt Weill *described prewar German society in popular theater music.*

George Gershwin, *composer-songwriter, introduced the soul of America to Europe.*

MODERN PERIOD
(1940 – present)

Contemporary, electronic, computer, and experimental music influenced by American jazz and Eastern music from India, Japan, and China.

COMPOSERS:

Bartók (1881–1945)
Ellington (1899–1974)
Copland (1900–1990)
Cage (1912–1992)
Britten (1913–1976)
Bernstein (1918–1990)
Ligeti (1923–)
Boulez (1925–)
Stockhausen (1928–)
Reich (1936–)
Glass (1937–)
Adams (1947–)

Béla Bartók *wove Hungarian folk songs into works for piano and orchestra.*

Benjamin Britten, *British composer-conductor, wrote operas, chamber music, and church music.*

Aaron Copland *brought America to life with his ballets and suites.*

Leonard Bernstein, *composer-conductor-pianist, crossed boundaries between classical & popular music.*

Philip Glass *uses rhythm, changing tones, & repetition in his minimalist music.*

German composer **Karlheinz Stockhausen** *created new music with tapes & electronic sounds.*

Diversity of Music

Every country has its own sounds, rhythms, instruments, songs, and dance.
The music reflects the culture and the people.
The diverse sounds have influenced both classical and popular music.

A Scottish bagpiper makes music by squeezing a bag of air.

The Chinese pi'pa sounds soft and clear.

Bands of primitive pipes and drums play in the streets of Bolivia.

Long Indian ragas are improvised on the sitar and tabla.

Some music sounds like noise to me.

Then you just listen until the sounds become familiar.

Music helps me understand the people who make it, even if they live far away.

Steel drum bands play calypso folk songs on used, tuned oil drums in the West Indies.

The didgeridoo, a tree branch hollowed out by ants and termites, has been played by Aboriginal Australians for 3,000 years.

Bells, gongs, xylophones, and drums make up a gamelan in Indonesia.

The expressive koto is a kind of zither played in Japan.

The African sansa has metal strips plucked with the thumbs.

The alphorn and accordion are favorite folk instruments in Switzerland.

The Birth of Jazz

In America, people immigrated from other countries and brought their cultures and music with them. JAZZ is the first uniquely American music.

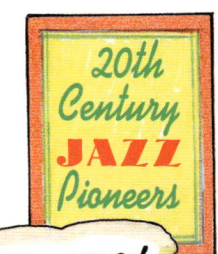

20th Century JAZZ Pioneers

Jazz has rhythm.

And feeling!

And great artists who improvise on the melody.

They are LEGENDS!

A MINI HISTORY

JAZZ grew out of many influences in the 1880s and 1900s: the songs of slavery, the musical scene in New Orleans, minstrel shows, the banjo, and others.

1800

In the South, spirituals, gospel church music, and work songs express the grief, despair, and hope during the dark period of American slavery.

Various conditions influence the birth of JAZZ:

- NEW ORLEANS—a lively city of mixed races, cultures (French, African, Creole, Caribbean), and music attracts talented musicians.

- Popular MINSTREL SHOWS with tambourines, banjos, and singers sweep across U.S. cities, entertaining with skits and songs.

- THE BANJO's plucky sound inspires the syncopated beat of JAZZ. Its origin can be traced to West Africa.

JAZZ springs up in the North, on the East and West coasts, and in between.

1900 New Orleans

Bouncy BRASS BANDS improvise music in the streets for funerals and carnivals.

RAGTIME hits Chicago

MAPLE LEAF RAG — Piano Rags By the King of Ragtime Writers Scott Joplin

RAGTIME composers introduce a popular syncopated beat in music.

Jelly Roll Morton and his Red Hot Peppers — Coast to Coast US TOUR TONIGHT

Popular RAGTIME pianist-composer is first to write down JAZZ music.

1900 Mississippi Delta

Robert Johnson, Ma Rainey, Bessie Smith, BB King, W.C. Handy, Muddy Waters

THE BLUES
Earthy music formed of certain "blue-note" chords reflects the melancholy mood of the time.

40

1920s
The Roaring Twenties
CHICAGO becomes JAZZ capital!
King Oliver, Johnny Dodds, Sidney Bechet, Kid Ory, Fats Waller

THE JAZZ AGE
Music reaches people via radio, gramophone, clubs, film, concerts, theaters, and dance. JAZZ unifies everyone.

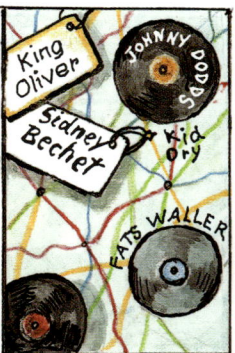

JAZZ artists travel through big cities, and DIXIELAND JAZZ catches on.

Django Reinhart, Hot Club, Stephane Grapelli

JAZZ becomes popular in France, then throughout Europe and Japan.

1930s
LOUIS — Famous Jazz Legends — Ella Fitzgerald, Billie Holiday

JAZZ bands travel to Europe along with brilliant singers and instrumentalists like Louis Armstrong, the ultimate JAZZ artist for the next 50 years.

1930s & 1940s
NEW YORK COTTON CLUB
Count Basie, Fletcher Henderson, Duke Ellington · Composer · Band leader · Pianist

Stan Kenton, Jimmy + Tommy Dorsey, Frank Sinatra, BENNY GOODMAN King of Swing, Paul Whiteman

BOOGIE WOOGIE

Bebop — Dizzy Gillespie, Art Tatum, Bud Powell, Thelonius Monk, Dinah Washington, Lester Young, Charlie Parker, Ray Brown, Sarah Vaughn

SWING ERA
Big Bands become favorites with dancers who swing with the music.

White JAZZ musicians emerge, and SWING becomes a craze in dance halls.

Dancers Lindy-Hop, Shim, Sham, Shimmy, & Jitterbug to records on the jukebox.

Talented JAZZ artists who will become legends reach enthusiastic audiences.

1950s & 1960s
NEW YORK CARNEGIE HALL — Jazz at the Philharmonic
Dvořák, Ravel, Schuller's Third Stream, Gershwin, Stravinsky, STORMY WEATHER with Cab Calloway, COMING SOON

JAZZ sweeps West Coast
Quincy Jones, Dave Brubeck, Charlie Mingus, Chet Baker, John Coltrane, Stan Getz, Sonny Rollins, Art Blakey, MILES DAVIS, Dexter Gordon, MODERN JAZZ QUARTET

Nat King Cole, Lena Horne, Billy Eckstine, Carmen McCrea, Ray Charles, Anita O'Day, Peggy Lee, Cleo Laine

1970s & 1980s
Keith Jarrett, Herbie Hancock, George Shearing, Chick Corea, Cassandra Wilson, Nancy Wilson, Diana Krall, Christian McBride, Wynton Marsalis, Marsalis Family

JAZZ influences classical composers and is celebrated in concerts, festivals, & films.

Unique JAZZ trumpeter influences new wave of COOL JAZZ, MODERN JAZZ, FREE JAZZ, FUSION, and ELECTRONIC JAZZ.

Great singers leave bands & enter a new popularity on records, stage, and radio.

After a slump, when other music becomes more popular, a JAZZ REVIVAL—led by Wynton Marsalis and others—brings old & new energy to JAZZ.

Then through the 1990s and into a new century, Jazz reaches a new generation of artists who look backward and forward. Jazz is CLASSIC!

And then comes... Turn the page for more.

I'm getting a headache.

Popular Music in a Small World

Music became popular with a bang.
It first spread by radio. Then by phonograph records, the jukebox, television, tapes, videos, compact disks, and LIVE concert tours.
Pop music filled the airwaves.
People mooned, swooned, danced, dreamed, tapped, snapped, wept, screamed, and clapped as they listened to their favorite music, performer, or group.

1920s
- Vaudeville
- Tin Pan Alley — Al Jolson
- Variety
- Music Halls
- Big Bands

1930s
Leadbelly, Pete, Woody, Gershwin, da Silva, Cole Porter, Jerome Kern, Irving Berlin, *Hillbilly, HOLLYWOOD, PORGY + BESS, Andrews Sisters

1940s
FRANKIE
- Ballroom dance
- Foxtrot
- Tango
- Rumba
- Samba
- cha-cha
Harold Arlen, Judy, Leonard Bernstein, BROADWAY

1950s
Lerner + Lowe, Rodgers + Hart + Hammerstein, OKLAHOMA!, Elmo Bernstein, Grand ol' Opry, Hank, Loretta, NASHVILLE, Willie Nelson, Tammy, Mountain, Delta

JAZZ ★ FOLK ★ Show Tunes ★ Ballads ★ MUSICALS ★ Country Western ★ Bluegrass

1955
Bill Haley, Buddy, ROCK around the Clock, Beau Jocque, Buckwheat Zydeco, Cajun, Zydeco, Creole, Beau Soleil, BooZoo, ELVIS

Johnny Mathis, Johnny Ray, Johnny Hartman, Perry Como, Mel Tormé, Joe Williams, The Mills Brothers, The Ink Spots, West Side Story, Sondheim

1960s
THE BEATLES — Paul! John! George! Ringo!
Ravi Shankar, Johnny Cash, Joan Baez, John Denver, DYLAN, Joni, Rolling Stones, Leonard Cohen, Dusty Springfield

New Orleans Sound ★ Rockabilly ★ Rock'n Roll ★ POP ★ Rock ★ Protest Songs ★ Folk Rock ★ Pop Rock ★ Country Pop

On and on it goes.
Pop music moves and changes with the times.
It reflects the popular trends of cultures and tastes.
Some of it will come and go, some will remain.
It is still going strong, and it is GLOBAL!

Music is Therapy

Everyone has a favorite kind of music that brings comfort and pleasure.
Music makes work easier in factories, in offices, or at home.
It inspires all kinds of artists who listen to music as they create.
Music is good for everyone.

Music helps tense people relax.	It helps babies fall asleep.	It helps sick people feel better.	It helps calm angry people.
Music cheers sad people.	Music helps people create.	It feels good to make music with friends.	

Some people like listening to different kinds of music while doing different things.

In the kitchen	In the workroom	In the bathroom

Music is Good for Animals, Too

I like Bach best.

It helps cows give more milk.

It helps hens lay bigger eggs.

It helps shy elephants perform.

Songbirds, whales, wolves, and other animals make their own kind of music.

Their song sounds inspire composers and others.

whale   dolphin   seal   wolf

Don't mind Boomer. He likes to sing along.

Even plants grow happy with a song!

Practice Makes Perfect

We make music.
Making music is hard fun.
It takes lots of practice to learn
to play an instrument.

But when you do, it is forever.

That's the hard part.

Here's the fun part.

As you practice and learn,
you begin to make
beautiful sounds.
Practice becomes fun.

You learn new pieces to play.
You feel proud.
Your music teacher says
you will play in a recital.
You will play for an audience.

A metronome
helps keep time.

The Performance

At your recital it is your turn to play.
Everyone is looking at you.

she must be nervous.

You concentrate.
You do the best you can.

When you finish, everyone claps.
It sounds like waves breaking.
It feels good. You take a bow.
You feel relieved and very proud.

You celebrate.
Everyone says you did well.
Next time it will be even
better, because you are
learning more every day.
Practice makes perfect.

Music is for Everybody

It is for anyone who wants to hear the sound, dance to the rhythm, clap to the beat, sing along, or be still to imagine....

I love music.

Me too. Ruff.